LILY OF MARY

ST. BERNADETTE OF LOURDES

VENERABLE SISTER MARY BERNARD

SENSUS FIDELIUM PRESS

To The Immaculate Conception, sole National Patron of America, who in these pages sends to American Catholics, through little Bernadette, a special message, which, if heeded, will solve every mission problem of America, this little book is filially dedicated with inexpressible love, by M.B., the Editor.

February 11, 1918, Feast of the First Appearance of the Immaculate Conception to Bernadette, which appearance occurred February 11, 1858.

CONTENTS

PREFACE TO THE AMERICAN EDITION

This life of Bernadette of Lourdes, called here "The Lily of Mary," carries a message to American Catholics from the Immaculate Conception, their National Patroness, which, the translator is convinced, contains the solution of the most important question before the American Church today—the mission question, and he has endeavored to bring this out and emphasize it in the following prefatory words.

A Message Of Our Blessed Lady under the Title of her Immaculate Conception Patroness of America, To American Catholics

The story of Bernadette of Lourdes is one of the most beautiful of all stories. It is a story which tells not merely of the most beautiful things of earth but one which mirrors forth in the fullest and most resplendent manner—as no other story does—the most beautiful of all the gifts of heaven—the Immaculate Conception of the Virgin Mother of God.

In the eternal mind of God, before the world was made, when the incarnation of the Son of God and the redemption of men were determined upon, the Immaculate Conception of the Virgin Mother of God was decreed in all its details. How God seems to have delighted in it! How He has poured out its resplendent and supernatural beauty on all that He has done for man in time and eternity!

The very first promise made by God to men was the promise of the Immaculate Conception. "She shall crush thy head," said God to Satan in the Garden of Paradise, speaking of the Virgin Mother. "Never for one moment shall she be under thy power and even in her conception, which shall be made immaculate, shall she begin thy complete overthrow."

When the incarnation of the Son of God and the redemption of men came to their actual fulfillment they were prefaced by the announcement of the Immaculate Conception with which their accomplishment began. "Hail full of grace"—that is, *immaculate* said the angel to the Virgin Mother of God.

Finally after 1900 years, when Pius IX decreed the Immaculate Conception to be an article of Catholic faith, the Virgin Mother herself appeared on earth to little Bernadette and after detailing and emphasizing in many ways that the work of the Immaculate Conception is to bring about the conversion of souls by prayer and penance and humiliation and every possible way marked out by God, she proclaimed, March 25, 1858: "I am the Immaculate Conception,"

"What is thy name?" asked the child over and over again in obedience to the parish priest. "My name," answered the Virgin Mother of God, "is the Immaculate Conception."

Her distinguishing name is not Mary—many others are thus called—but the name she received from God in eternity, before the world was—the name by which she will be

distinguished from all other creatures for ever and ever—
the name which no other creature will ever be able to claim
—I am the Immaculate Conception.

The revelation to Bernadette seems to emphasize still
further the meaning of the decree of Pius IX, which
proclaimed indeed that the Virgin Mother of God was
conceived without sin, but did not explicitly declare, as the
revelation to Bernadette seems to imply, that the Immaculate Conception is her peculiar name whereby she is distinguished from all other creatures.

"I am who am," said God, "that is my peculiar name
which no other being can claim."

"I am the Immaculate Conception," said the Virgin
Mother of God to Bernadette, "that is my peculiar name
which no other creature can ever possess."

The story of Bernadette of Lourdes is the story of the
Immaculate Conception blossomed in full amongst men in
the course of time—brought out in the most wonderful and
beautiful and touching manner possible. But what should be
especially emphasized in this story, and yet is often lost sight
of, is what the Immaculate Conception herself chiefly
insisted upon—the message regarding conversions which she
gave to Bernadette. This message was not a single, isolated
message, but rather a series of messages all converging to the
one point: Pray and work for conversions. Observe, too, that
though the child besought her again and again to give her
name the Virgin Mother constantly refused, and for a
number of days, until she had reiterated and emphasized her
message in many ways. Not until she had done this would she
proclaim: I am the Immaculate Conception. As if she would
say: I am indeed the Immaculate Conception, but the peculiar office and work of the Immaculate Conception, which
must be insisted upon and for which it was decreed by God,

is to bring about the conversion of souls and therefore to have all make use of the means of conversion—prayer and work of every kind ordained by God for conversion.

Pray and work for the conversion of the countless souls now perishing—this is the message which the Immaculate Conception gave to little Bernadette and bade her convey to all.

What amongst us in America should be chiefly insisted upon is that it is a message of the Immaculate Conception to American Catholics above all and has special application at the present time to their work in foreign missions.

First of all understand that in the providence of God the sole National Patron of America is the Immaculate Conception. What does that mean? It means that the one being whom God through the appointment of His church has made the Protector, the Leader, the Model of America and Americans in the battle against Satan is the Immaculate Conception. How can it be possible that God should give to America the Immaculate Conception for its sole National Patron and that the greatest and most wonderful and important message of the Immaculate Conception should have no particular interest for America? Are we not justified in concluding—are we not forced to conclude—that of all people on earth American Catholics are most bound to heed and obey that message?

Some say that America is the sole nation on earth that has the Immaculate Conception for its National Patron. But if this be true—and it seems certainly true—does it not greatly emphasize the point in question?

In the second place, the message of the Immaculate Conception, whilst laying down the duty of praying and working for the conversion of all souls without God's grace must in the nature of things have particular reference to praying and working for the salvation of those souls that stand in the greatest need and form the greatest number. But there are no people on earth who can compare with the pagans in point of numbers and wretched spiritual destitution. The pagans form two-thirds of the whole human race —nearly 1,000 million souls—and they are beyond question in the most destitute spiritual condition possible. If, therefore, there are any people on earth who constitute a special object for the exercise of the message of the Immaculate Conception it is surely the almost countless millions of wretched pagans.

Besides all this, the pagans are just at this time in a condition more favorable for their conversion than at any former period of the 1900 years of Christianity. Up to a few years ago Catholic missioners were largely prevented from working in pagan countries by the most terrible persecutions, but in recent times Western commerce and civilization have penetrated all the pagan lands and done away with all the barriers of exclusiveness and persecution. For the first time in 1900 years Catholic missionaries are free to spread Christianity without hindrance among the countless millions of Japan and China and India and Africa. Just before the great war began the Church was taking advantage of this opportunity, pouring in her missionaries and supplies amongst the pagans as she had never done before, and the conversion of the pagans was going forward by leaps and bounds. Over one million were under instruction to enter the Church at the opening of the war and the only reason why there were not five million or ten million was simply that the Church did not have the missioners to send into the work. Never in all the 1900 years of her existence had the Church so glorious a prospect for the conversion of the pagans.

But the great war began and, sad to relate! of all the havoc it has wrought the saddest is the ruin it has brought to the missions. Great numbers of the missionaries were drafted into the European armies and the missions were left in the hands of the older missioners. Heroically these older missioners have been struggling, but they have been unable to keep up the work and daily their ranks are thinned by sickness and death. The poor Catholic missions are now going down every day. No new missioners are coming from Europe: the seminaries there are practically all closed and for many, many years this dearth of missioners must continue. Not only has the great war taken away the missioners, but it has cut off missionary efforts of almost every kind from almost all the nations except America. Today America is almost the only nation on earth in any sort of condition to help the missions. One thousand million pagans today are in a sense appealing to America for salvation.

Could there possibly be a time when the message of the Immaculate Conception should be more heeded by us?

Publisher, 2024: Although the specific circumstances encountered by the author in 1918 do not exist today in relation to World War I and seminaries, the need for conversion in the world has certainly never been greater.

But there is another reason why this message of the Immaculate Conception should enforce itself upon American Catholics.

We are the wealthiest nation on earth. Nothing has

brought this out so clearly as the present war. The financial efforts of any other of the nations, gigantic as they may have been, seem almost like the efforts of pigmies compared to ours. Nowhere else on earth do wealth and the luxury of life appear as in America. But we are paying and must pay more and more the penalty for all this luxury and worldliness. Day by day our Catholic life is going down perceptibly under the corrupting influences surrounding us. To this all who have had anything to do with the care of souls in America will testify.

To resist these corrupting influences, to keep our Catholic life pure and untainted, to spread our Catholic faith throughout America, there is no possible way except to build up and increase among our people the apostolic spirit. It is this apostolic spirit that has established the Catholic Church and maintained it and spread it throughout the earth during all the ages. Where it decreases or fails among our people the Catholic Church infallibly weakens or becomes extinct. Where it increases the Catholic Church infallibly waxes strong and goes forward. The apostolic spirit is the one great vital force in the Catholic Church on which all else is dependent.

But the carrying out of the message of the Immaculate Conception is the means whereby we can beget and maintain and increase the apostolic spirit among our people and solve our every mission problem. Make our people realize that message, fill them with a burning, consuming spirit of carrying it out, train them into practices and habits of sacrificing themselves to aid the salvation of the countless souls now perishing and we shall soon make our people an apostolic people and save both the numberless wretched pagans now perishing and our own people in so doing.

Nor let this be thought a hopeless task and a utopian

delusion. At this very time we behold our luxurious, plea-sure-loving Americans throwing everything aside for the sake of country and casting themselves by the millions into the most murderous war the world has ever seen. Will our American Catholics sacrifice less to save our own people and the countless souls in pagan lands from eternal destruc-tion? We will not believe it.

A faint picture of what we can do in this respect we have thrust constantly before our eyes—a picture that should put us to shame to doubt our capabilities. Some years ago—and not so many—the Protestants around us did nothing for missions, hardly sent out a missionary or gave so much as a penny for mission work, but by educating their people to the mission idea the mission work of Protestants today covers the earth. They send out thousands and thousands of missioners and they give millions and millions for their support. We are more numerous than they, we are stronger than they, we have a thousand times the motive that they have for this work, and if we but hammer into our people, in season and out of season, this message of the Immaculate Conception we will have a thousand times greater results than the American Protestants.

Besides all this we have for the training of our people into mission work a means the most powerful conceivable and one which Protestants have never even dreamed of— our parochial schools. In our parochial schools there are a million and a half of children—almost a whole generation of American Catholics—material enough if properly educated to furnish missionaries for the world and to support all the missions of the Church. Educate that vast army of children in the message of the Immaculate Concep-tion, train them into practices and habits of continually praying and sacrificing themselves to aid the countless millions now perishing eternally and we will soon have an apostolic nation that will send out missionaries to the whole world.

Let, therefore, the message of the Immaculate Conception, our sole National Patron, be our cry till our people be consumed with a burning desire to realize it, till our children are fully educated and trained in the practice of carrying it out, till it becomes the air we breathe, the sole meat we eat, the motive of our every action. Then shall we have a generation of missionaries, then shall we fill the earth with our mission work, then shall we solve our every mission problem at home and abroad, then shall we people heaven with the millions of souls now rushing into hell.

"Pray and work for the conversion of the countless millions now perishing—I who send this message by little Bernadette to you, my American children, am the Immaculate Conception, decreed by God to crush the head of the Serpent, destined by God through the appointment of the Church to be your sole National Patron, to be your model, to lead you in battle against the forces of hell. Follow me. Pray and work for the conversion of the countless millions now perishing."

M. B., Feb. 11, 1918.

NOTES

In connection with this "Message of the Immaculate Conception" we have issued some cards containing a formula of resolution to be signed by those who wish to join in the resolution of carrying out the injunction of our Immaculate Mother to become missionaries to the countless souls now perishing by praying and working for their conversion. These cards read as follows:

Would you wish to join in the resolution to carry out this message?

If so, please sign the following:

O, Mother Immaculate, Patron of America, I hereby sign my name to join in the resolution to carry out your message conveyed through little Bernadette, to become a missionary throughout my life to the countless souls now perishing, by praying and working for their conversion and especially do I resolve to say every day one Hail Mary or other prayer and to do such work or works, for their conversion as I may choose according to my circumstances.

Signed..

Address..

The cards also contain the following prayer approved by his Eminence Cardinal Farley:

A DAILY PRAYER

According to the Message of the Immaculate Conception

O, Mother Immaculate, Patron of America, who through little Bernadette, bade us pray and work for the conversion of the countless souls now perishing, I offer up all the prayers, actions and sufferings of this day and every day of my life for their conversion and I beg of thee to bless my resolution to do what I can throughout my life to bring about their salvation.

HAIL MARY.

We have been urged to bring out this short life of Bernadette for three reasons: First, because in these days there are thousands who will not read a large book, but who will be glad to have a short attractive story, and in the case of Bernadette, who is one of the most celebrated and attractive characters in the Church of today, it is thought that such a life would receive an unusual welcome.

In the second place, the fact that Bernadette bears from our Immaculate Mother a message to all Catholics, but especially to American Catholics, on the most important matter before the world today—to pray and work for the conversion of the countless souls now perishing—and the fact that Bernadette not only bears this message, but is the living exemplification of it in life and death, make us believe that the bringing out of her life in a short attractive form at this time is a matter of very great importance and is likely to bear great influence upon the salvation of many souls.

A prayer to obtain favors from the Immaculate Conception, Patron of America, for the glorification of Bernadette has been authorized by the Roman authorities. It has special reference to American Catholics.

[The following prayer can be used, either in novenas, or otherwise, to obtain favors, especially of conversions, through Bernadette. With it can also be used, in imitation of Bernadette, the Rosary, some penances and Lourdes water.]

Prayer To Mary Immaculate, Patron of America, To Obtain the Glorification of Bernadette

O Mary Immaculate, who for so long a time hast protected thy American children, loving them with a special love, remember that, by choosing little Bernadett. out of all the earth to proclaim to the world that thou art the Immaculate Conception, thou hast united the name of this humble child of France to all that America holds most sacred. Glorify, we beseech thee, little Bernadette, so that after having made her the confidante and messenger of thy

Immaculate Conception, thou shouldst deign still to choose her as the instrument of the graces and favors of which America stands in such great need.

Grant me the grace which my heart desires at this moment and grant it through the intercession of Bernadette, so that it may be more and more evident that thou lovest this privileged child with a particular love, and that from heaven above, thou desirest that the Church should honor her memory and propose her as a new model to be imitated, a new protector to support us in the sorrows of life and help us to arrive at eternal beatitude. Amen.

O Mary Immaculate, aid the cause of little Bernadette, thy humble child!

O Mary Immaculate, protect the work of Bernadette for the conversion of sinners!

Nihil Obstat: Carolus Salotti, S.C.Adv.

Sacra. Rit. Congr. Assessor.

Publisher, 2024: St. Bernadette was canonized by Pius XI on December 8th, 1933.

LETTER TO THE AUTHOR

OF RT. REV. PETER CHATELUS, BISHOP OF NEVERS

✠ Nevers, June 17, 1914.

My dear daughter:

Two years have passed since I blessed your book, entitled "La Confidente de l'Immaculée."[1] Today you offer me your "sketch": The Lily of Mary, Bernadette Soubirous, Venerable Sister Mary Bernard. This new work is a short but faithful account of the life of Bernadette.

Lourdes, Bartrès and the apparitions are made to pass before the reader's eye rapidly, but in a very striking manner. You then show Bernadette at Nevers in the cloister, as a mystic lily, exhaling the perfume of a soul filled with the love of the Holy Eucharist and our Immaculate Mother. You conclude by briefly relating the history of her apostolate and sufferings.

This abridged account of the life of Bernadette of Lourdes and the Sister of Charity of Nevers, is very interesting and will be welcomed by those who desire a short life of the privileged child of Mary.

Your pages, breathing the sweet and heavenly soul of

Bernadette, are written with a pen which expresses itself in the most attractive and suitable manner. I bless the work and predict for it a success equal to that of the larger work which has already been translated into several languages and spread throughout the world.

My dear child, accept my congratulations and the expression of my devotion, in our Lord.

✠ Peter, Bishop of Nevers.

THE LILY OF MARY

Te elegi.
I have chosen thee.
(Aggeus 2:24)

1

THE CRADLE—LOURDES—BARTRÈS

On the seventh day of January, 1844, at the Boly Mill in Lourdes in the Lapaca quarter, Francis Soubirous and his wife Louise Casterot, bending over the cradle of their first angel, who had just been given them by heaven, rejoiced in the happiness of this blessing bestowed upon their home, and poured out their hearts in thanksgiving to God. If they had been able to read the future, what holy joy would have animated their gratitude! And if the ear of their soul had been open to celestial harmonies sung around that crib, how thrilling had it been to hear,

In low-breathed chants unknown to earth,
The love of heaven for this flower,
Who ravished even at her birth,
The love of Mary and her power.

On the ninth of January the Curé and Dean of Lourdes, Father Forgue, poured the holy waters of Baptism upon this child. She received the name Mary-Bernard (Marie-Bernarde) which afterwards was turned for short into the familiar diminutive, Bernadette. In the month of July, Louise, who was awaiting another angel, being obliged to put Bernadette out to be nursed, confided her to Marie Lagues Aravant, wife of Mr. Aravant of Bartrès. This true Christian woman was just then mourning an infant son whom God had taken to Himself. Upon the child of the Soubirous, she lavished all the care and affection of her heart, and after fifteen months brought her back home. This was in the month of October, 1845.

At this time Bernadette's family were in comfortable circumstances; but whether it was that Francis Soubirous was not very careful, or was a poor manager, or that Louise, sweet, polite and above all hard working, had more heart than spirit of economy, the income of the mill became less day by day, and soon want made itself felt in this honest, but improvident, home.

The time came when Francis, having lost his mill and having moved from house to house, was unable to pay rent any longer and was obliged to seek the charity of one of his relations, Andrew Sajous, who permitted the Soubirous family to lodge in a house which he owned in the Rue des Petits-Fossés. This was in fact the old jail of Lourdes and bore the name "Cachot."

Bernadette grew, but her health was always frail. Very early in life asthma, from which she suffered as long as she lived, made its appearance and afflicted her at times to such an extent, that she would faint from the intense suffocation it produced. Her parents did for her all their poverty permitted them. In the place of maize bread, which was the ordinary food of the family, they bought her some wheat bread and sometimes even a little good wine which they sweetened with sugar.

During the winter of 1855, which was very rigorous in the Pyrénées, Bernadette's Aunt, Bernarde, asked to have her little godchild live with her. For seven or eight months, she kept Bernadette in her family, and treated her with the same affection as her own children. Bernadette returned home and remained there till the summer of 1857. Bartrès had not been forgotten. Marie Aravant visited her every little while, and brought her fruit, or cakes, or some other little remembrance. On her side Bernadette always remained fondly attached to her foster mother whom she went to see several times in the year.

Towards the end of 1857, Marie Aravant asked the Soubirous to let her have Bernadette to take care of the children. Bernadette's parents, knowing that at Bartrès their daughter would be treated as one of the family, willingly consented to the change, but the Aravants instead of confiding the care of the children to Bernadette, gave her charge of the sheep, chiefly the lambs.

Thus Bernadette passed her days upon the hillsides surrounding Bartrès. She could neither read nor write, but she knew better than anyone around her that marvelous book of the rosary and very often poured forth her pure, simple, unaffected soul in the recitation of the Our Father, the Hail Mary and the Creed.

In the silence of nature, this virgin lily shed its perfume among the wild flowers of the field she loved. These flowers she often formed into crowns, and offered them to her Mother in heaven upon the little altars which she made from stones collected here and there.

> Her Aves sweet and countless rise
> Like songs to heaven—chanted sighs
> Which angels' golden harps repeat
> Before our Mother's mercy seat.

Yes, this child so upright, so pure and so simple was truly a sister of the Angels. Her modesty and openness of heart had impressed the Curé of Bartrès, a priest of unusual intelligence, piety and zeal. "If the mental picture which I have drawn of the children of Salette is true," said he, one day to the Superintendent of the Public School, Mr. Barbet, "this little shepherdess must surely resemble them."

These words were held as a sort of prophecy.

But the piety of Bernadette did not prevent her from taking good care of her sheep, and heaven, as if to bless her efforts, deigned to reward her. It is related—and the facts are vouched for by credible witnesses—that one day when the little shepherdess had conducted her flock to the pasture, a storm suddenly burst forth. The elder Aravant, who from his house could see Bernadette on the side of the hill, beckoned to her to come back at once. To gather her sheep took some little time. The road below the village is crossed by a brook which at that time had no bridge over it except a simple plank for pedestrians. When Bernadette came to this stream, which in the morning she had passed over without difficulty, she found it greatly swollen. It had overflowed the two sides of the road, and it was impossible for the sheep to pass through it. Troubled and anxious, the child made the sign of the cross and suddenly the waters divided: the oncoming waters became suspended and the others continued to flow, leaving a dry passage over which Bernadette and her sheep crossed, after which the waters immediately resumed their natural course.

In spite of her suffering condition, Bernadette was always joyful and smiling. Mr. Aravant was known to be stern and at times even hard and close. But the child never complained of anybody or anything. She was obedient to all, gave no trouble, took what was given her and was content with everything.

Bernadette had reached her fourteenth year, and still had not made her First Communion. She felt, however, a strong desire to receive our Lord and asked her parents to bring her back home, "because she wished to return to Lourdes to make her First Communion."

In the beginning of the year 1858, she came back to her home in the Rue des Petits-Fossés. Though poor, this home did not lack nobility: a truly Christian spirit, union, mutual love and respect made it rich and honorable. The children, morning and evening, gathered around their parents, knelt before God and offered to Him as so much incense placed upon the altar, their thoughts and resolutions, their desires and above all their hearts. Thus the love of heaven over-shadowed this home and spread around it, even in its poverty, an atmosphere of peace and secret happiness. But the time was at hand when the dark clouds which hung over it were to be brightened under the influence of Our Lady.

THE HEAVENLY VISION

Lourdes, at the time we write, was a small picturesque village of the Pyrénées, peaceably seated in its solitude on the banks of the Gave which chants a perpetual song, in the shadow of the surrounding mountains and of the ancient walls of its Saracenic Château. On the side of the ancient mass of rock which is found at the west of the village, nature has cut out a grotto the depth of which is not sufficient to prevent the light from flooding it. Everything around is buried in profound silence.

In murmurs deep, the Gave alone
With chant eternal wakes the vale,
While nature smiles with arms outthrown,
To hear the Heavens impart their tale.

FIRST APPARITION
THURSDAY, FEBRUARY 11TH

On the eleventh of February, 1858, at noon, the hour when the Angelus sounded from all the church steeples in the Pyrénées, Bernadette with her sister Toinette and Jeanne Abadie, one of their little neighbors, went to gather firewood on the left bank of the Gave and in doing so, passed through the field adjoining Massabielle. The Gave was low at that time and a small, dry bank of sand and pebbles was formed between two streams. The waters of a canal (which emptied then into the Gave in front of the grotto, and were utilized for turning a mill) were not strong that day for the mill was not then running. But let Bernadette speak for herself, and tell the story of the first apparition in all its simplicity; a story which has been found written with her own hand in her private notes:

"The first time I was at the grotto I went to gather wood with two other little girls. When we were at the mill I asked them if they would like to go and see where the water of the canal emptied into the Gave. They answered me: yes. From there, we followed the canal, and found ourselves before a grotto. Not being able to follow the canal further, my two companions crossed the water in front of the grotto. Then I found myself alone on the side opposite them. 'I asked the two others if they would help me throw some stones in the water to see if I could not pass over without taking off my shoes: they told me to do as they had done, if I wished. I went a little further to see if I could not pass over at some other point without taking off my shoes, but it was of no use. Then I came back before the grotto. Scarcely had I taken off my first stocking, when I heard a noise as of a mighty wind. I turned my head and looked across the field, but I saw the trees perfectly still. I continued taking off my shoes and stockings, when I heard the same noise again and as I raised my head to look at the grotto, I saw a lady in white. I was somewhat dazed and, believing that I saw before me an illusion, I rubbed my eyes, but in vain. I continued to see the same lady. Then I put my hand in my pocket and took out my rosary. I wished to make the sign of the cross, but I was not able to raise my hand to my forehead. The shock was too much for me. The lady took the rosary which she was holding in her hands and made the sign of the cross. I then tried a second time and succeeded. As soon as I had made the sign of the cross, the great fear which had seized on me vanished, and I knelt down and said my rosary in the presence of the beautiful lady. After saying the rosary, she made me a sign to approach, but I did not dare; then she disappeared.

After taking off my other shoe and stocking, I crossed the little stream in front of the grotto and then we went away. On the road I asked my companions if they had not seen anything. "No," they said to me, "and you—have you seen something?"—"Oh, no; if you have seen nothing neither have I." I did not wish to tell them, but they begged me so hard, that I finally decided I would if they would keep the matter secret. They promised to do so, but no sooner did they get home than they hastened to tell what I had seen. This happened February 11th, 1858."

Bernadette's account goes no further, but we know that her mother, fearing her daughter was being tricked by some illusion, forbade her to go to the grotto again. Her motherly solitude was still more alarmed when Bernadette, under strong emotion, burst into tears on saying the evening prayers and so she renewed her prohibition. "We went to bed," said the child, "but I was unable to sleep. The sweet, beautiful face of the Lady came back to me continually, and in spite of all my mother had said, I could not believe that I had been deceived."

4

SECOND APPARITION
SUNDAY, FEBRUARY 14TH

In the meantime supernatural and irresistible attraction drew Bernadette to the rock; but how to overcome the opposition of her mother?

On Sunday, February 14th, after High Mass, five or six young companions of Bernadette, desirous of going with her to the grotto, begged her mother to let her go. At last she gave way to their entreaties, not, however, without making the most pressing injunctions. Passing before the church, the little group provided themselves with holy water and at length reached the rock of Massabielle. There solitude and silence reigned. They all knelt down and began to say the rosary. "She is there!" suddenly cried Bernadette, "She smiles!" The face of Bernadette shone brightly. She went forward and threw holy water towards the Vision, saying: "If you are from God, come forward." The lady smiled again and approaching, bent towards the child, who knelt down and passed immediately into ecstasy. A stone thrown from the heights above the grotto did not disturb her. So great a change had come over the little shepherdess that her companions were filled with the greatest anxiety. Marie, her sister, believed that she was about to die. They tried to rouse her from her ecstasy. The miller, Nicholau, at last took her away, though he, too, was awed by her supernatural condition. During the whole time the Mysterious Being held herself before Bernadette. At length the Vision disappeared and Bernadette came to herself. In the meantime, her mother had been informed of matters, and arrived disposed to punish her daughter, when the wife of Nicholau, who had seen the child in ecstasy, stopped her, saying, "Do not strike the child. Your daughter is an angel." From that time the thought of the Lady possessed Bernadette. She contemplated her as she had appeared in her wonderful beauty with a grace and a majesty which the child found it impossible to express. Later on she will have only disdain for all human comparisons. Before women of the world, distinguished and brilliant, she will cry out, "Oh, they can bear no comparison. My own Lady is beautiful, far more beautiful than any of them."

Here is a description made up from the details given by Bernadette herself: "The Blessed Virgin wore a dress of dazzling whiteness gathered in graceful folds high against the neck. The sleeves were close fitting. Her head was covered by a veil which went down to the forehead, then following the contour of her body and falling upon her shoulders and barely touching her arms, it dropped in graceful folds on both sides to the feet. A blue girdle encircled her waist. It was without a knot and floated before her, large and plain and much below the knees. Her feet were bare and could just be seen under the last folds of her dress, and on each foot was a full-blown yellow rose. From one of her arms hung a long rosary the beads of which were dazzling white; the chain was of shining yellow and the crucifix was yellow like the chain."

5

THIRD APPARITION
THURSDAY, FEBRUARY 18TH

On the eighteenth of February, at daybreak Bernadette accompanied by Mrs. Millet and Miss Peyrot, a Child of Mary, went to the grotto after hearing Mass. This time the group had provided themselves with a blessed candle as a defense against Satan, and they also had a sheet of paper, pen and ink so that the person who was appearing at the grotto might put in writing whatever she desired.

With astonishing agility, Bernadette, in spite of her asthma, outstripped the others in reaching the grotto. When they arrived, Bernadette cried out, "She is there!" and the child gave herself up to the contemplation of her whom she found so beautiful and attractive and "whom she dared to love." She went forward to the wild rose bush at the foot of the niche and raising herself to her full height she besought the Vision to put her desires in writing. The Vision replied: "What I have to say to you it is not necessary to write. Would you have the kindness to come here for fifteen days?" And as the child answered quickly in the affirmative she added: "I do not promise that you will be happy in this world, but in the other."

Bernadette was absorbed in prayer, which she interrupted from time to time in order to hold secret converse with the Vision. This lasted one hour, then the Vision disappeared.

6

FOURTH APPARITION
FRIDAY, FEBRUARY 19TH

When Bernadette's mother saw how peaceful and happy her daughter was, her fears began to give way. What Bernadette told her of the heavenly beauty and the gentle sweetness of the Lady made her trust that there was no Satanic illusion. She therefore persuaded her husband, Francis, to allow Bernadette to go to the grotto during the fortnight.

The request of the Vision to Bernadette had not been kept secret, and when on the morning of February 19th, Bernadette, accompanied by her mother and her aunt Bernarde, reached the grotto, a little caravan was with her.

The child knelt down, raised the crucifix of her rosary to her forehead and made the sign of the cross. The next moment the material world, so far as she was concerned, had disappeared. Her soul was plunged into ravishing ecstasy. Her whole being thrilled with joy. She smiled and smiled to the Vision to whom her soul seemed about to fly. Her mother, seized with amazement and fear, cried out, "O my God! I beg Thee not to take away my child." Some people in the crowd exclaimed, "Oh! how beautiful she is!" The rapture lasted about half an hour. It was a half hour of heaven.

7

FIFTH APPARITION

SATURDAY, FEBRUARY 20TH

The little group at the grotto, on the morning of February 19th, was only the forerunner of "the crowds of Lourdes." The rumor of the apparitions spread not only in the little capital of Bigorre, but to all the surrounding villages. The name of Bernadette was on every lip and the humble child became the engrossing topic of conversation of the whole neighborhood. Some laughed at her, others made it a point to remain indifferent, but many even then conjectured the name of the Lady.

From all sides the crowds came. At first they could be numbered by hundreds, but soon they grew into thousands. Bernadette passed through the crowds seemingly unconscious of them. "I saw nothing," she declared later on to a nun; "so much was I absorbed in the thought of the Lady."

She was accustomed to kneel upon a rock which was always held in reserve for her. "It is Bernadette's place," everybody said. She said the rosary with her eyes fixed upon the niche. Soon her face became transfigured, and the crowd, awed by the presence of the supernatural, which they could not explain, sought for the invisible upon her face which had become possessed of an incomparable charm.

At this fifth apparition, during which the ecstasy lasted forty minutes, Bernadette declared that the Lady had taught her word for word a prayer for herself alone. What was this prayer which came from the heart of God's Mother? No one else ever knew, but the faithful little disciple herself declared that she repeated it every day of her life.

8

SIXTH APPARITION
SUNDAY, FEBRUARY 21ST

Coming to the grotto at six o'clock in the morning, Bernadette was greeted with enthusiastic acclamations to which she paid no attention. On that day, the humble child was destined to convert a distinguished physician, Dr. Dozous, to a belief in the supernatural. He had decided to come in person to Massabielle in the secret hope of demolishing with a word, in the name of science, all this childish display of neurotic mysticism. But a mere view of the ecstatic made him understand that here was a case beyond the powers of ordinary medical science. When he had satisfied himself that Bernadette, whilst in ecstasy, kept full possession of herself, that several times, when the candle was extinguished by the wind, she passed it to a neighbor to be relighted, that her pulse was normal, the circulation of her blood regular and that there was no nervous excitement, he felt that the finger of God was here. However, before giving in, he came back several times to Massabielle—we shall see him there again—and later on he will be found "one of the most ardent champions of our Lady of Lourdes." The doctor during this sixth apparition, noted that the countenance of Bernadette was suddenly struck sad and two tears rolled down her cheeks. It was because "the Lady" for a moment had gazed sadly into the distance, then looking again at the child kneeling at her feet, she said to her: "Pray for sinners." Heavenly joy soon again beamed from the countenance of the Vision, but the words she had uttered fell deep into the heart of Bernadette and ever afterwards held a large part in her life.

SEVENTH APPARITION
TUESDAY, FEBRUARY 23RD

Bernadette went to the grotto after Holy Mass on the 23rd. Suddenly she seemed born to a new life and her eyes shone with a heavenly light. Angelic smiles played upon her lips, mysterious conversations took place between her and the heavenly Being who ravished her out of herself. At one time in the attitude of a listener, she thrilled with joy and happiness, at another suppliant and humble and moved to tears she seemed to pray. It was the apparition of the "secrets." Mary raised the humble child to the sublime role of confidante and thereby bound her to her heart by a "triple secret" which Bernadette carried to the grave.

This time a second conversion took place in the person of Mr. Estrade, a tax collector of Lourdes, who was locally credited with a superiority of intelligence and wit. With Doctor Dozous, also present at this apparition, he felt that the time for philosophizing was past and that the hour for veneration was at hand.

10

EIGHTH APPARITION
WEDNESDAY, FEBRUARY 24TH

U p to this time the Lady of the Grotto had only spoken intimately to her child. She absorbed her, she fashioned her to her desires, she prepared her for her mission, and by the prodigy of her repeated ecstasies she disposed people to receive her who, having now been elevated to the role of confidante, was to go forth as her messenger to the whole world.

At the eighth apparition the scene was enlarged and even in the midst of her raptures. Bernadette in tears and sobs repeated to the crowd the words she heard from the mouth of the heavenly Lady: "Penitence, Penitence, Penitence!" After the child of her heart, the Heavenly Mother went immediately to the children of her mercy, to sinners, whom she exhorted to repent, to do penance, to obtain the pardon of heaven.

NINTH APPARITION
THURSDAY, FEBRUARY 25TH

This is the day on which the heavenly Lady caused to burst forth the miraculous spring which was destined to rejoice the city of Mary, to increase faith, to confound science, to assuage grief, to work cures, to purify and give life to souls as well as to bodies. But in order to open this new Pool of Siloam to the world, the Mother of Mercy made use of the humiliation of her child: "Go to the spring, drink and wash there," she said to Bernadette in ecstasy. Bernadette went to the river, but on a sign from the Vision she looked around puzzled and anxious. She then raised her eyes to the niche again, as if to consult the Vision once more, after which she came to the left corner of the grotto. She then dug the earth with her fingers. Immediately the little hole she had dug filled with muddy water. After making three attempts she drank some of it. Then she washed her face with it, after which she plucked a blade of grass and ate it. A tiny stream of water soon appeared, flowing from the hole which Bernadette had dug. No one could doubt that this spring from the Massabielle rock was a gift from heaven. The sick of the whole world later on were to declare its power. Confidence in Bernadette (which had been shaken by the humiliating acts she had performed) was once again established and the Lady more exalted than ever.

12

TENTH APPARITION
FRIDAY, FEBRUARY 26TH

When Bernadette came to the grotto she expressed no surprise at seeing the new spring. She made the sign of the cross, then drank some of the water of the spring and again bathed her face with it.

This day the heavenly Lady wished to make Bernadette go still further into the mystery of reparation. She was already enjoying the bliss of ecstasy when she heard these words: "Kiss the earth for sinners." At once the humble child bent down and kissed the ground. Then, doubtless by inspiration, she called upon all present to do likewise. The supernatural radiance of this child, commanding upon her knees, produced amazement and hope. Now, it was that God appeared under these mysterious events: now, it was that Mary was about to put forth her mercy. Massabielle was to become the grotto of the Transfiguration.

13

ELEVENTH APPARITION
SATURDAY, FEBRUARY 27TH

B ernadette, according to her promise, continued her visits to the Lady of the Rock during the fortnight. On the morning of the 27th her joyful intercourse and contemplation were prolonged more than usual. Then, said Bernadette, the Lady seemed to assume an air of recollection and meditation, after which, breaking the silence, which is always a prelude to great things, she spoke the words: "Go and tell the priests that a chapel should be built here." The child after the ecstasy appeared much troubled. The thought of meeting the stern Curé made her tremble. "He is good indeed," she said, "but I fear him more than a gendarme." Screwing up her courage, however, she went to the presbytery. We should say here that the Curé of Lourdes, Mgr. Peyramale, was "a man of high stature, commanding presence and stern countenance—manly, open, energetic and with a heart as true as steel."

He had taken no part in the events of the grotto, thereby giving an example of prudence, which was followed by the other clergy of the town. He left to Divine Providence to pronounce upon Bernadette's visions and waited.

The Curé received Bernadette coldly and, in the conversation which ensued, he put forward every possible objection and did not hesitate to make use of irony; but Bernadette, child as she was—humble, timid and ignorant —answered him so respectfully, firmly and satisfactorily, that he was astounded. At his request Bernadette gave him all the details which had taken place up to that time. And as she spoke, the stern priest was overcome with emotion. He saw before him a soul "as clear as crystal" and a secret instinct made him recognize the Mother of God under the features of the Lady of the Grotto. But he kept his feelings to himself and replied: "Child, you shall say to the Lady who sent you, that the Cure of Lourdes is not in the habit of dealing with people whom he does not know, that first of all, she must let him know who she is, and then, that she must prove that she has a right to the name she claims. If this Lady has a right to a chapel she will understand my words, and if she does not understand them, you will tell her that she can dispense from sending any more messages to the Curé."

Bernadette raised her pure eyes to the Curé, made her little country courtesy and took her departure.

TWELFTH APPARITION
SUNDAY, FEBRUARY 28TH

On February 28th, more than two thousand persons had arrived at the grotto before Bernadette. She came with her Aunt Lucile. Immediately a mass of human heads was packed closely around her on both sides of the river banks. In the midst of this living amphitheater, the angelic figure of the little country girl shone with supernatural splendor, for the Lady did not delay her visit. The mysterious intercourse of this day was purely private. Mary was doubtless preparing her child for her future mission. When the ecstasy was ended, Bernadette desired to go to the rock as usual, but she found it impossible to advance on account of the dense crowd. Two soldiers of the fort, who were present, forced of their own accord, a passage for her. "Make way," they cried. One of them turning to his comrade said in barrack slang: "And they tell us the apparition is a fake! By Heavens! if any of the hayseeds on my mess say anything to me about it, they had better look out."

THIRTEENTH APPARITION
MONDAY, MARCH 1ST

B ernadette had consented to use at her next visit to the grotto the rosary of a pious friend who had requested her to do so. But when she began to say the Hail Mary, using this rosary, the Blessed Virgin stopped her. The child immediately took out her own rosary and presented it to the Lady and again commenced her prayer.

Ever since Bernadette had directed the people around her to imitate her in kissing the ground for sinners, most of those present at the apparitions imitated her in her acts of piety at the grotto. When, therefore, they saw Bernadette present her rosary to the Vision they did the same, making a perfect ovation. When Bernadette came out of the ecstasy, she explained the reason of her act. Those who had imitated her had the comfort of being disillusioned, but the Blessed Virgin had read correctly the heart of her people.

FOURTEENTH APPARITION
WEDNESDAY, MARCH 2ND

Prayer, transfiguration and spiritual delights followed one upon the other and were blended together in this fourteenth apparition. Bernadette, however, arose from her ecstasy in a visibly anxious state of mind. Not only had the Lady of the Grotto repeated her injunction to go and tell the priests that they should build a church at Massabielle, but she added: "I wish that processions should come here."

Such was the message which the humble child was to convey to the Curé who gave her "a cold welcome," she wrote later. She begged her Aunt Basile to go with her. Her Aunt had little more courage than her niece. "Whenever I meet that holy man," she said, "my limbs tremble and my flesh creeps with fear." However, she consented to go to the presbytery with Bernadette.

When the Curé heard the word "processions", he could hardly restrain himself. He demanded that the Lady of the Grotto should give a sign that she had a right to what she asked. A sign, a miracle! What were then the transfigurations of the little peasant, the pouring out of the crowds, the conversions brought about, the cures wrought by the water which had spontaneously burst forth under the hand of the child!

The humble Bernadette had laid bare the sacred spring which was to work cures upon the body. Her word was to cause a sanctuary to rise upon the rock where souls will find life in forgiveness, prayer and the Holy Eucharist. The redeeming powers which from Massabielle were to descend upon the world might already be foreseen.

17

FIFTEENTH APPARITION
THURSDAY, MARCH 4TH

On the morning of March 3rd, Bernadette prayed piously at the grotto but gave no sign of ecstasy. The next day was the last of the fortnight, and it was hoped that some striking prodigy would close the wonderful events of the grotto. More than 20,000 pilgrims assembled to see the child in ecstasy, to hear from her mouth the will of the mysterious Lady, and to learn her name, perhaps, for she had not yet revealed it. When Bernadette started from home in the rue des Petits-Fossés, she was preceded to the grotto by two gendarmes with drawn swords to open a way for her, and to prevent the crowds from pressing upon her. Always modest and simple, absorbed already in the thought of the Lady, she passed along quietly, "very natural because she was supernaturalized."

As soon as she commenced her prayer, every voice was hushed, every knee bent, and emotion stirred every heart. The scene was not delayed and the ecstasy lasted nearly an hour, but nothing miraculous took place at the grotto. The expectations of many were then disappointed, but the Lady in quitting little Bernadette had not said adieu. She had smiled as usual, but had no intention of leaving her work unfinished.

18

SIXTEENTH APPARITION

THURSDAY, MARCH 25TH

The fortnight of the apparitions had passed, but Bernadette came back very often to Massabielle and, when she could, she spent happy hours contemplating in spirit the Vision which had enraptured her. A rustic altar, flowers, lights and prayers had transformed the place into a sanctuary and already alms were being left at the grotto for the chapel to be built.

Three weeks had passed and the eve of March 25th came. A secret attraction drew pious souls to the grotto to celebrate the feast of Mary on the morrow, but how much stronger was that attraction in the heart of Bernadette! She recognized in it the accustomed call of the Vision when she desired to appear —sweet and pressing—and the desires of the child hastened the hour of the visit.

In the evening, at the family circle, she spoke of her joy and her hope, and she passed the night without sleep but not without happiness.

The Hail Mary, a thousand times repeated, ravished the heart of the divine Mother, who prepared for her child on the next day a feast more glorious than any which had preceded, and so ardently did she desire the meeting that she was at the grotto in advance of Bernadette. Sweet, smiling and flooded with light, she awaited the child. Bernadette, filled with confusion, asked pardon for her tardy arrival. She was reassured and an hour of heaven began for her. Never had the Lady appeared so tender and so encouraging and the child, recalling that she had never yet told her name, asked her twice: "Madame, would you be kind enough to tell me who you are?" A smile was the only answer, but it was a smile of such sweetness that Bernadette asked her a third time, yet more beseechingly. Then the lady, standing as usual above the rose tree, assumed a grave and humble expression. She joined her hands, raised them to her breast and looked up to heaven; then separating her hands slowly and bending towards the child pronounced these words:

Que soy era Immaculado Conception I am the Immaculate Conception.

Then, without a glance and without a word of farewell, she disappeared, leaving Bernadette her image and her name.

The mystery of the grotto was revealed. The little shepherdess heard the name which the Blessed Virgin had received in the secret counsels of God before she was born and called Mary. Bernadette, however, did not understand the significance of the name she had heard, and, in order not to forget it, she kept repeating over and over again all the way to the presbytery: Que soy era Immaculado Conceptiou.

The Curé, however, understood, and so did all the faithful. A wave of enthusiasm rolled over the city. The grotto, the blessed rock, and the branches of the rose bush, became so many relics which were kissed with reverence and love. It was truly **SHE** who had appeared—**SHE** whose name had been spoken with awe—the **Queen of heaven—Mary, full of grace!**

19

SEVENTEENTH APPARITION
WEDNESDAY, APRIL 7TH

On March 25th, the Blessed Virgin came to give her name to the world. On April 7th, she came to place upon that name the seal of a miracle. On the morning of that day, when Bernadette was praying, absorbed in ecstasy, she drew her right hand to her left, in which was a lighted candle and immediately the flame of the candle was seen to pass between her fingers. "She is burning herself," those around her anxiously cried. But Bernadette remained perfectly unmoved. Doctor Dozous, whom Divine Providence had brought there to be present at this prodigy, prevented the extinguishing of the candle, though a current of air was blowing the flame continuously upon Bernadette's fingers. This lasted a quarter of an hour. Not only did Bernadette not feel any pain, but her hand showed no trace of any burn. After the ecstasy, the Doctor wished to try the opposite experiment. Several times he placed the flame of the candle to her left hand and Bernadette quickly drew it aside, saying: "You are burning me."

This was the token of the last apparition which the

public was to witness. Bernadette, however, was to see Mary once again.

20

EIGHTEENTH APPARITION

FRIDAY, JULY 16TH

Three months went by and the privileged child of our Lady had the happiness of receiving Our Lord in Holy Communion for the first time. This event took place in the chapel of the Hospice. "Bernadette made her First Communion yesterday," the Curé of Lourdes wrote the next day to Mgr. Lawrence, Bishop of Tarbes, "and she appeared much penetrated with the greatness of this act. During the retreat which I gave to the children, her conduct was perfect. Everything in her is developing in a wonderful way." It was Innocence approaching the banquet of angels, and augmenting its purity by contact with infinite purity. Bernadette was asked which occasion had made her happier, receiving her First Communion or her intercourse with the Blessed Virgin at the grotto. She said, "I do not know. These things go together and are not to be compared. What I do know is that I was happy on both occasions."

On July 16th she had received Holy Communion for the third time and at the end of that day, so filled with devotion to the Holy Eucharist and to the Blessed Virgin, she felt in the depths of her heart a call well known to her—the call of her Immaculate Mother to the grotto. She arose and with her Aunt Lucile hastened to the meeting. The civil authorities had prohibited at that time any access to the grotto and they had shut off the front by a palisade of boards. Bernadette and her Aunt, therefore, went to kneel on the other side of the Gave in front of the grotto. It was evening, at the hour when the bell of the parish church was about to ring the Angelus. Suddenly the child cried out, thrilled with joy, "She is there! She is there! She greets us. She smiles to us above the palisade!" The palisade disappeared from the eyes of Bernadette, and she saw only her heavenly Mother, ineffably tender. Once again the child was lost in ecstasy and love. She received no farewell word—the heart of her Mother could not bear to speak it—but a glance and a smile of such tenderness that Bernadette declared she had never seen the like. That glance, that smile, she was never again to see except in heaven.

21

FROM THE GROTTO OF THE VISION
TO THE CLOISTER

The breath of the Holy Spirit drew souls to Lourdes. There Mary established the most brilliant of her thrones and there she formed the most magnificent of her courts. There the innocent child, whose soul was as pure as the waters of the Pyrénéan springs, was to be her witness.

After the apparitions, Bernadette had left the school of the Sisters of Nevers (annexed to the Hospice) and was no longer to be found in the "Cachot" in the Rue des Petits-Fossés, but at a mill hidden at the foot of the Fort. Here she was overwhelmed by visitors, who thronged to see her and hear her and ask her questions. She was always simple and modest, and told and retold in spite of her asthma the wonderful story of the grotto. This she did with such an air of truth that her words never failed to carry conviction to the unprejudiced. Concise and luminous, straight to the point, wonderfully apt, and most so when sudden and unforeseen objections were made, it was clear that heaven spoke through the mouth of this humble child.

For some time she remained at home, but the Curé of Lourdes, M. Peyramale, wishing to keep her to some extent from importunate visitors, with the concurrence of M. Lacade, Mayor of Lourdes, asked the Superior of the Hospice to receive her. The Sisters gladly welcomed the privileged child of Mary, but they did not let her suspect their happiness. There, as at her own home, visitors came to see her from all parts—France, Spain, Italy, etc., and it may be truly said that seldom did it happen that anyone left her without having received greater light in his soul and deeper love for the Immaculate Virgin in his heart.

Father Ollivier, a Franciscan, asked one day for the favor of an interview with Bernadette: "I do not think I was prejudiced," he said, "but I had always been on my guard against views accepted without reason and against first impressions. I was not moved by curiosity; I had a desire of personal conviction in this matter. But while Bernadette was speaking, I was overcome by a sweet and powerful feeling which took away the possibility of resistance. There seemed to come forth from Bernadette a light and a sweetness that went to the bottom of my soul. I had the same impressions as those who were present at the apparitions and ecstasies. I had the irresistible intuition of a mysterious Being which the child saw with the eyes of her soul after having seen it with the eyes of her body. It is impossible to speak of beings not really present as Bernadette spoke of the Immaculate Mother. An indefinable dignity enveloped the child as she spoke. She seemed like one of the angels of the Scripture relating to men the secrets of God. After thirty years I have yet before my mind's eye the radiance of that child, in my ear the sound of her voice and in my heart the penetration of her grace."

"It was neither beauty nor charm as ordinarily understood. It was innocence and modesty in fullest attraction, with an indefinable delicacy and finish borrowed from contact with the ineffable purity of Mary. I think I make myself understood, though I cannot express what I feel."

One of the scenes of the apparitions—that of March 25th—strongly impressed everyone who saw Bernadette reproduce it. The famous sculptor of Lyons, M. Fabisch, who had accepted the task of trying to reproduce in marble the beauty which had enraptured the child, wrote: "I have never seen anything so beautiful as her action when I asked her how the Blessed Virgin looked as she said, 'I am the Immaculate Conception.'

"She rose with great simplicity, joined her hands and raised her eyes to heaven, but neither Fra Angelico nor Perugin nor Raphael ever executed anything so sweet and at the same time so full of depth, as the look of that poor, simple and unaffected little girl. I shall never forget, as long as I live, her heavenly expression. I have studied in Italy and elsewhere the masterpieces of the great artists, of those who have excelled in portraying the expression of divine love and ecstasy, but in none of them have I ever found so sweet and ravishing an expression, and every time I asked Bernadette to re-enact the scene, always the same expression changed, illumined and transformed her countenance so that it made me weep with emotion."

And what this celebrated sculptor experienced in the endeavor to reproduce an ideal he was unable to attain, everyone who had the happiness of seeing her also experienced and left her, saying: "She had undoubtedly seen what she reproduces; it is of heaven, not of earth."

It belonged to the Church, however, to judge of Bernadette's apparitions. After four years of searching investigation, in which study and prayer were diligently resorted to, Bishop Lawrence, of Tarbes, wrote in his decree of January, 1862: "We judge that the Immaculate Mary, Mother of God, did really appear to Bernadette Soubirous, on February 11th, 1858, and the days following to the number of eighteen times in the Grotto of Massabielle, near the town of Lourdes; that this apparition bears all the characters of truth, and that the faithful are justified in holding it certain." On the other hand miracles gave their testimony to the truth of the heavenly vision. Louis Bourriette, a stone cutter of Lourdes, who had lost one of his eyes when blasting, recovered the fullness of his sight on applying the water of the spring, whilst it was still muddy. It was significant that the first cure should be that of a blind man. The Blessed Virgin seemed to say: I come to bring light. Let those come forward who doubt. I wish to make of Massabielle a radiant centre whence I shall spread over the whole earth the light of faith and hope.

The white statue of the Madonna had been cut out from a great block of Carrara marble. It was ready, and M. Fabisch had told Bernadette: "When you see it, I wish you to say, 'It is She'!" Then he placed it before her eyes and anxiously awaited the words of Bernadette on his masterpiece; but Bernadette said in a low voice: "It is beautiful, but it is not She. . . . It differs like earth from heaven." Bernadette had seen "what no genius could see, what no human heart could understand."

The blessing of the statue, the first ceremony at the grotto, took place April 4th, 1864. On this occasion several thousands of pilgrims and a great number of priests assembled with the bishop at their head.

"The voice of the Priest of God for the first time resounded among the rocks which had heard the voice of Mary. The orator of the day, filled with the inspiration of the occasion and the holiness of the moment, gave a voice to things around to salute and applaud the loved Beauty who had come to make her abode in the niche of the rocks."

The crypt of the Basilica was blessed and opened to divine service on May 21st, 1866. This was the first response to the request of the Blessed Virgin: "Go and tell the priests a church should be built here"; but soon the summits of the mountains became clothed in the vesture of Mary; the stones were transfigured into a basilica, whence hymns arose echoing to the cry of hosanna, which sets out from the far mountains and to the vivat of glory which rises from every torrent and valley and proclaims the conquering love of the Immaculate Conception."

Did Bernadette foresee these triumphs for her Heavenly Lady? She has not said it, but she was at the source of all this expression of glory. She had repeated the words of the Blessed Virgin, and her words formed a sort of creative germ of life, whence afterwards everything at Massabielle blossomed into love. This was a glorious day indeed for the Queen of Heaven, but Bernadette, always humble, tried to hide herself among the Children of Mary of her parish. Everyone, however, wanted to see her, to touch her, to take something belonging to her. People went so far as to cut off bits of her veil. "We were obliged to surround her," said one of the nuns, "to prevent her clothing from being taken from her." "The Saint! See the Saint!" was heard on all sides. The pious child suffered much from these manifestations. The more she was exalted, the more she humbled herself. "You look upon me as though I were some curious animal," she said.

∼

THE CHILD OF FEBRUARY 11TH, 1858, had seen with her own eyes, near the place she had fallen upon her knees, a bishop at the altar. She had heard the acclamations which had greeted the name of the mysterious Lady who had appeared to her. She was then able to follow the voice which called her to the solitude of the cloister. In August, 1864, Bernadette manifested to Mother Alexander Roques, the Superior of the Lourdes Hospice, her desire of being received into the congregation of the Sisters of Nevers, but her state of health kept her two years longer at Lourdes. During that period her lung troubles were so critical that the Last Sacraments were administered to her, and her death was expected shortly, when she suddenly asked for some Lourdes water. As soon as she drank it, she declared herself cured. "I felt as if a mountain had been lifted from my chest," she said. Bernadette followed the exercises of the community just as if she had been a nun. She longed for the time when she would be able to obey the call of the divine Master.

"Oh, my dear Mother," she wrote, on April 28th, 1866, to the superior of Puéchabon, whom she had known at Lourdes, "how I long for the great day when I shall have the happiness of entering the novitiate, for it must surely be heaven on earth."

On July 4th, 1866, Bernadette tore herself away from Lourdes, her family and the grotto—"which was her heaven on earth." She went to Nevers. The Lily of Mary was to blossom in all its fullness in that atmosphere and there to shed forth her sweetest perfume.

22

THE GARDEN ENCLOSED

B ernadette had been the faithful messenger of the Immaculate Virgin, and near the grotto, where heaven had been opened to her eyes, she had heard in the depths of her soul, a voice full of power and sweetness, saying: "Come and follow Me."

Her soul o'ercome by this appeal divine,

To Jesus said: "Henceforth I will be Thine."

Then sped she to the promised land and fair,

A land where lilies sweetest perfume bear.

But where was this "Land of Promise"? What was this "garden enclosed" chosen by Mary, in which to transplant the Lily of her heart? The "Land of Promise" was Nevers, as we have said, and the "garden enclosed" was the novitiate of the Sisters of Charity and Christian Instruction. This land was impregnated with Benedictine life and, at the time when Bernadette knocked at the door, the congregation was in full vigor, not only in regard to its spirit and its life of prayer, but still more in its development of charitable works. The son of St. Benedict had realized the plan which the

divine Master had shown him in the silence of contemplation, a plan which detailed the manner in which the
subjects called to the institute should employ themselves in
carrying on the work of God's harvest. It seemed that our
Lord had made him hear these words:

By penitential practices and prayer
Some spread the peace of holiness around;
While others make the children's souls their care,
That youthful piety may more abound.
And some, as heralds of my mercy great,
Announce to fallen man the boon of grace;
From sick and dying and disconsolate
My cross doth every claim of hell efface.

50,000 children received christian education in their
numerous schools or convents, and 40,000 sick were nursed
either in hospitals or at home—"grace" and "mercy"
obtained not only by prayer and the sacrifices of each, but
above all by the crucifixion of those souls, whom God chose
for Himself as victims in the solitude of the infirmary. These
are they whose sole mission seems to be "to diffuse holiness." We shall see later that it was the mission of
Bernadette after she became Sister Marie-Bernard. The
Congregation at this time had at its head Reverend Mother
Josephine Imbert, who was endowed with remarkable
wisdom, and such energy that in spite of continual suffering,
she was able to carry out all her duties. Her virtue was most
attractive and she was large-hearted, compassionate and
firm.

The Mistress of Novices was the Reverend Mother
Marie-Therese Vauzou. She, too, was a woman of
extraordinary character, high minded, broad and of superior intelligence. She brought to the mission God assigned

her a double passion, which dominated her—the love of Christ and the love of souls—and she possessed a wonderful tact for molding those who came under her direction.

She saw in Bernadette a treasure confided to her. Her spiritual instinct caused her to place Bernadette in a hidden life of silence, mortifications and humiliations of every kind, so that her companions in the novitiate were astonished at the continuous and severe trials to which she was subjected, and at her ever humble and joyous submission.

On July 29th, Bernadette had the happiness of receiving the religious habit, and with it the name of Marie-Bernard. Clothed with the livery of Christ, the young virgin hid herself still more in the solitude of her cenacle. "I came here to hide myself," she said, and all unanimously declared that she seemed to have only one ambition to be forgotten and be accounted as nothing. Each of the novices in her own way lauded her perfect regularity, her simplicity, her obedience and charity. A mysterious charm about her spoke silently of God, and her virtue appeared so natural and amiable that it seemed to be without effort.

Sister-Marie-Bernard always retained her artless simplicity, childishness, if I dare say so, which is the clothing of innocence. "Do you skip here," she asked a few days after her arrival at the novitiate. "No, but our recreations are happy." "Oh, I delight in turning the rope for others to skip."

Three months after entering the novitiate, the young novice was in danger of death and, after having received the last sacraments, made her religious vows with angelic fervor. But it seemed that God had brought His faithful servant to this extremity only for the purpose of hastening the divine alliance. Scarcely had she made the gift of herself to God when her health was restored. Then in the intensity of joy into which she was plunged by this grace, which in her humility she had not dared hope for, believing herself unworthy to become a member of the Institute, she took in her hands the crucifix and the nun's veil, which are given to the professed sisters. "I hold these," she said; "they are my own. I am a member of the congregation and no one can now send me away." At once she resumed the exercises of the novitiate. She tried hard to conceal her virtue, saying, "I am like everyone else." Her companions admired her and considered her their guardian angel, though they were very careful not to let her suspect it, otherwise the mission which she carried on without being aware of it, would never have been fulfilled.

At recreation she was charming. One day, placing herself between two of the tallest novices, she said, "See how little I am! How could I ever think anything of myself?"

Everything spoke to her of God. He was her all. Passing near an apple tree, she exclaimed, "How I hate those apples! They remind me of original sin." And at another time, "How pleasant those grapes are! They make me think of our Lord's blood."

During this year of novitiate the divine Master was pleased to give her a heavy cross to bear. Her mother, who seemed unable to endure life after the departure of her daughter, went to heaven to contemplate our Immaculate Mother, whom her child had already seen on earth. Keenly did Sister Marie-Bernard feel this loss. But "fiat" was her first word: "My God, you have wished it. I accept the chalice you have given me. May your holy Name be blessed!" Thus the grace of suffering had prepared Bernadette for her religious profession. She made it with all her companions,

October 30th, 1867. Thence she was given up to her divine Spouse and she was able to sing:

> I live on faith, I live on love,
> On gratitude to God above.
> A sacrifice, I make of me.

23

THE THING OF GOD, I THAT SHALL BE.</CENTER> FRAGRANCE OF THE HIDDEN LIFE

T he privileged child of Mary had sought the solitude of the cloister "in order to hide herself," and the Superior General desired to leave her fully in this silence—this blessed atmosphere of the Mother-House. There she was to shed the perfume of the violet upon those who had the happiness to come in contact with her.

Humility! Mary seemed to cover her child with it as with an armor. Bishop Lelong, on the day of her funeral, thus praised this virtue in this young virgin: "You are my witnesses, sisters, that no one hid her. She hid herself and yet not sufficiently to satisfy her desire. How she loved this blessed retreat! How she dreaded going out of it! How she feared that, after quitting the world, the world would come to her! And her striking humility, too, amidst honor extorts our admiration and praise. Has not St. Bernard said that this is so rare a thing that no human soil can produce a plant so precious"?

To a superior, who asked if she had not felt some temptation of self love in having been so favored by the Blessed Virgin, she replied: "What idea can you have of me? Do I not know that if the Blessed Virgin chose me it was because I was the most ignorant of all. If she had found another more ignorant than I am, she would have chosen her in my place."

"One day, when she was in the infirmary," relates one of her companions, "I showed her a picture of the Grotto of Lourdes, and while she was looking at it, I cast my eyes upon her with a kind of veneration. Did she see what I did? Likely, for she immediately asked me: "What do you do with a broom?"

"What a question! Sweep with it."

"And then?"

"Put it back in its place."

"Where is its place?"

"In the corner, behind the door."

"You are right, and that is my life. The Blessed Virgin made use of me, then she placed me in a corner. That is my place. I am happy in it and there will I remain."

"Two days after my arrival at Nevers," wrote another nun, "I expressed to the Superior my sorrow at not yet having made the acquaintance of Bernadette. Just then there was with me, near the Reverend Mother, a very young sister, and she said to me, "Bernadette! Why there she is!" Probably I had pictured to myself a less simple ideal of Bernadette, and an unbecoming word, almost contemptuous, escaped me: "That!" Immediately with a natural and charming gesture, the humble novice gave me her hand and smilingly answered me, "Yes, indeed, it is only 'that!'" The embarrassment I then felt comes to me again when I recall this incident which humbles me and exalts her."

Here is a prayer which Bernadette, on May 12th, 1866, addressed to the Blessed Virgin: "Yes, O tender Mother, you have stooped even to earth, to a weak little child, to communicate to her certain things in spite of her unworthiness.

And what reason had she not for humiliation? You, the Queen of heaven and earth, made use of what, according to the world, was the weakest of things. O Mary, give to her who dares to call herself your child, this precious virtue of humility. Make, O tender Mother, your child imitate you fully in everything. Make me, your child, according to your own heart and that of your beloved Son."

At Nevers, she had asked as a favor not to go to the parlor. When she was obliged to go there, it was a sacrifice for her, and her distress showed itself for a moment upon her extremely sensitive features. But she went immediately in obedience, and no matter who her visitor might be, she always appeared very simple and very modest. Because she was humble, Sister Marie-Bernard spread around her a spirit of fraternal charity in its every form—I was about to say in its every charm, for her charity was like a revelation—the blossoming of the life of Jesus in her soul.

During her long and painful illness, she was much grieved if she saw anyone deprived of sleep to nurse her. She begged earnestly of her superiors that only those might take care of her whose sleep would be sound enough to prevent their being disturbed by her sufferings.

"Sleep in that armchair," she said to a sister who was sitting up with her, "I will call you when necessary." And again: "Do not trouble yourself so. You yourself are probably more in need of the care you are giving me."

She encouraged, consoled and even reproved others, gave charitable advice, and this with so much simplicity and modesty that, without knowing it she became for each of the sisters one of those springs of which the Holy Spirit speaks: "Their life is always being poured out." In the same way from the heart of the humble nun, there incessantly escaped those expressions of divine love causing "oil and wine to be poured into wounds," as did Jesus, without pref-erence of person, or, like her Master, attaching herself by preference to the poorest, the most afflicted or those most in need."

For some time after her profession, Bernadette filled the office of infirmarian. "She took care of the sisters with admirable tact," said a nun. "When she came to the bedside of a sick person it seemed like the apparition of an angel of charity, so much sweetness was there in her encouragement, such peace and consolation did she bring."

The ecstatic of the grotto always remained poor. At Lourdes, visitors, moved with compassion at the poverty of the Soubirous family, had tried with all the delicacy and discretion of persons who know how to give, to make them accept assistance. Some money was secretly left on the mantle-piece or table, but the child gave it back immedi-ately. "One would have thought that money burnt her." And her parents imitated her in this disinterestedness, which was almost heroic.

This poverty Sister Marie-Bernard practiced in the minutest details when a nun. Never very particular in what was for her own use, she considered everything too good for her. And this detachment extended to the satisfaction of taste, of desires, and of her entire being. At meals, she left what was most agreeable to her, and took what best united her to God by mortification.

But it was the lily of purity which shed forth its perfumes to the fullest in this atmosphere of the hidden life. The purity of Sister Mary Bernard was reflected fully in her deep and limpid look. That alone of itself bore witness that she was the worthy daughter of the Blessed Virgin who had spoken to her. This virtue shone in her as a diamond without blemish. "He who has a pure heart will have the king for a friend." It was this purity which drew down upon Bernadette the favor of our Immaculate Mother. It was this virginity of soul, which made her find God, in the secret depths of an interior life. Hence she was able to say, "I place my joy in being a victim of the heart of Jesus; union, intimate union with Him, such as St. John had, by purity and love."

These perfumes pure, O humble little flower,
Thou hast exhaled where God has placed thy bower;
And here we find rayed forth in thy sweet light,
Thy candid soul as clear as crystal bright.

24

HER DEVOTION TO THE BLESSED SACRAMENT AND TO MARY

What can be sweeter or more profitable than to chant the ineffable canticle of Eucharistic wonders in the soul, to listen to Divine secrets revealed in the silence of prayer and to lovingly taste the sweetness of such thoughts in a soul become the little "host" of Jesus. Here the little "host" is Sister Marie-Bernard. She is also pure white. "Towards the end of October, 1876," relates a nun, "as I was conducting Sister Marie-Bernard to the infirmary, after listening to a sermon from the chaplain of the novitiate, she said to me:

"Oh, how happy that sermon has made me!"

"But why? The priest spoke of sin."

"Yes; but did you not hear what he said?"

"What then?"

"The priest said that no one committed sin except when he wished to commit it. Now I cannot remember ever having wished in my whole life to commit a sin, and hence I have not committed any. That is what makes me happy."

We have already seen that Bernadette, when at Bartrès, asked to come back to Lourdes, in order to make her First

Communion. Her pure soul felt the divine attraction of the Holy Eucharist and when, on June 3rd, 1858, Jesus responded to her appeal, the Curé of Lourdes was able to write to Monseigneur Lawrence, Bishop of Tarbes: "Bernadette appeared much penetrated with the holy act (receiving her First Holy Communion). Everything is developing in her quite wonderfully."

At Lourdes, when anyone wished to obtain a special grace, Bernadette was sent to pray at the foot of the tabernacle and it was said that her prayer was always heard. It was there she opened the heart of her Divine Master.

Often, when critically ill, she refused to take anything soothing during the night, which would have deprived her of Holy Communion the next day. The love of the Holy Eucharist was alive in her soul, and when the Curé, Father Peymale, once beheld her at Holy Communion with a halo of light around her head, what was it but a sign of her intimate union with Jesus? It is above all in a pure soul that Jesus blossoms in fullness and exhales His fragrance. At Nevers, during long and frequent visits to the Blessed Sacrament, her recollection was profound. She loved the divine atmosphere near the tabernacle, which envelopes the soul in supernatural light and silent love, and in order to isolate herself still more from her surroundings, she was accustomed to draw her veil forward on each side. "It is my little chapel," she would say.

After Holy Communion, her countenance was all illumined. At times, her face, bathed in tears, seemed transfigured. She used to remain a long time at her thanksgiving. "It is especially on my communion days," she wrote to the Mother General, then at Rome, "that I pay my debts of gratitude. My soul is filled with strength and confidence in thinking that it is not I who pray, but Jesus in me." Often prevented from attending Mass during the last years of her life, she loved to unite herself in spirit with all the Masses being celebrated in the world, and this she did by means of an engraving which represented the perpetual offering up of the Holy Sacrifice. "The picture has only the little altar boy present and with this I am not satisfied," she would say; "he never rings the bell."

Once on a feast day, when a party of novices paid her a visit, she expressed the happiness she felt during her hours of sleeplessness in uniting herself with our Lord. Then showing a little gilt monstrance attached to the curtains, she said, "The sight of this gives me the desire and strength to immolate myself when I feel more than usually isolated and suffering."

The Eucharistic life is a hidden life, a life of annihilation, carried out in silence and prayer and renunciation. Is not this the whole life of Sister Marie-Bernard? Her soul possessed habits truly Eucharistic.

"After the example of Jesus, and for the love of Jesus, I will carry the cross hidden in my heart with courage and generosity. For the love of our Lord, I will generously accept privations, sufferings and humiliations, as did Jesus and Mary, to glorify God." And if a soul devoted to the Holy Eucharist, is a soul devoted to the spirit of immolation, let us consider this: "O Jesus, give me, I pray Thee, the bread of patience to bear the trials which I suffer. O Jesus, Thou wishest me to be crucified: Fiat." "Give me the bread of strength to suffer well, the bread which will enable me to see Thee alone always and in all things."

Bernadette was truly a soul devoted to Mary. Who has ever belonged to Mary more completely than this child, whose purity drew upon her the gaze and the pleasure of the Queen of Heaven? Not only does the Immaculate

Mother make Bernadette her apostle and evangelist, but she deigns to raise her to the role of "confidante." The secrets which little Bernadette kept profoundly buried in her heart, without permitting even a word to escape her, which could cause them to be suspected, were like a sacred contract which bound the child to her Mother. And what a Mother! Let us say also, what a child! for we may well believe that Mary did not communicate herself to Bernadette till she had elevated her to herself by illumination and love.

Already upon the hillsides at Bartrès, the Ave Maria formed the divine bond of union between the heart of the Blessed Virgin and the heart of Bernadette. At Lourdes we have seen her recite this prayer—we might say, sing it in her soul—at the foot of the blessed rock. The nuns of the hospice often came upon her suddenly, when she was saying the rosary in the silence of their chapel, and at Nevers the sisters looked upon it as a favor to kneel with Sister Marie-Bernard at the feet of the Blessed Virgin to recite the Angelus. Her rosary and her sign of the cross were her sole sermon. How many victories have they not won for the Mother of God! Bernadette had left Lourdes, but she declared that every day she made in spirit her little pilgrimage to her dear rock.

The second chaplain of the community, on his return from the festival of the coronation of the Lourdes statue, obtained permission from the Superior General to give an account to Sister Marie-Bernard of this solemnity, which was a triumph for our Lady. "Bernadette's face shone with joy," he said, "when I spoke to her of that demonstration and of that outpouring of France and the whole world to the grotto. When I had finished the story of my pilgrimage and had told all that could interest her, she looked at me, with a simplicity and angelic candor, and said: 'What could I have done in all that crowd? I was indeed much better off in my infirmary!'" These admirable words clearly show the humility of her soul. Yes, let Mary be made known and be loved on earth, but let her little favorite child be always forgotten, unknown, contemned! These were the sole aspirations of her soul!

"Oh!" she said at times, "love her?" If people only knew how good she is! Say your rosary well; put yourself under her protection; you will never do so in vain."

One day when someone showed her a picture of a child on the Blessed Virgin's knees, looking up at her with joy and happiness, Sister Marie-Bernard was much moved and, casting an indescribable look upon the picture, she said: "It is thus that we should be always with the Blessed Virgin—as a child with its mother."

It was truly her own story. The heart of Mary was her home on earth. It was from that heart she drew strength and courage in temptation, in suffering and in difficulty.

"O my mother," she wrote, "may my heart, lost in yours, have no other love than the good pleasure of my divine Master." "May I commence here below the union of my soul with your soul, and glorify our Lord by the perpetual homage of perfect submission." But the hour approaches when Sister Marie-Bernard will contemplate in heaven the Immaculate Virgin of whom she said: "She is so beautiful, that when anyone has seen her once he would die to see her again."

25

APOSTLE AND VICTIM

Bernadette had turned to the world. She had related what she had seen, she had repeated what she had heard and her word, because it was the word of the Immaculate Mother, possessed such apostolic strength, that it raised up the world and cast it at the feet of her celestial Lady.

Consider the following:

"Go to the priests and say that a church should be built here, and gold and marble and precious stones draw together and chant one harmonious song to their Queen, and prayer has great temples for its quiet aspirations or its triumphant outbursts.

"I desire people to come here," and a thrill responds from all parts of the world. Seas and mountains form no obstacles; waves of pilgrims flow to the banks of the Gave, an army of souls gather together, the atmosphere is embalmed with prayer, the supernatural is felt and breathed and hovers above the crowds; all peoples find themselves united in the eternal Ave Maria and this union proclaims the unity, the vitality, the fecundity of the Church; Lourdes becomes a centre of Catholic life and the name of the Vicar of Jesus Christ is never pronounced there without eliciting enthusiasm and applause.

"Go to the *spring* and drink and wash there."

The wonderful spring bursts forth under the hand of the child and a magnificent outpouring of miracles proclaims the power as well as the goodness of Mary.

But the divine Mother calls souls to her feet only to give them to her Son, and Lourdes becomes a fruitful centre of Eucharistic life. We could imagine ourselves under the eastern sky in the bosom of a new Judea. Jesus is there in the Host; the priest carries Him in the monstrance, showing Him in the midst of the crowds, and thousands of voices acclaiming Him, "Hosanna to the Son of David; blessed is He Who cometh in the name of the Lord!" Then are heard cries of anguish and of grief and of confidence: Jesus bends to His people, the sick rise up, the paralytic walk and the blind open their eyes to the light.

"*Pray for sinners.*" This request, made by the Mother of God, was the dominating thought of Bernadette's life. Her sisters in religion have received it as a precious legacy, and a confraternity of prayer for the conversion of sinners, through the intercession of our Lady of Lourdes, has been established in the chapel of the mother-house, which witnessed the loving and suppliant prayer of the child of the grotto, who became Sister Marie-Bernard.

Apostle. Bernadette fulfilled this role in the bosom of her family, where she was the guardian angel of her brothers and sisters; later, by correspondence, charming in its simplicity and filled with affection and supernatural wisdom, she continued to counsel and encourage her sisters and brothers, and help them to bear the cross when laid upon them.

And who can express the love with which she enveloped her hidden and powerful apostolate of prayer and suffering? Her celestial Lady said to her: "I do not promise that you shall be happy in this world but in the other." The word of Mary to the child of her love was truly a preparation for her role as "victim." "It is without doubt a great suffering not to be able to breathe freely," she said one day, when tortured with asthma, "but it is much more painful to be tortured with interior suffering. *That is terrible.*" She never permitted another word on this subject to escape her—which is very significant.

The advice of her director, given in her private notes, reveal more fully a martyrdom of heart, but she had heard the words of the Blessed Virgin, "Penitence, Penitence," and when she felt sorrow overwhelm her, she said: "What folly to recoil when our Lord desires to nail our hands to the cross. The more I am crucified, the more I will rejoice."

Besides her interior martyrdom, she was afflicted by the trial of a nature full of life, but rendered helpless from sickness. She was extremely active and was always working at something, even on her sick bed. She had desired to devote herself especially to the sick or children, but looking at everything with the eyes of faith, she wrote: "My soul rejoices to have one trait of likeness to Jesus—to remain hidden in helplessness." "I must be a victim," she again wrote.

One day a Superior visited her on her bed of suffering and said: "What are you doing there, little Idleness?"

"My dear mother, I am doing my work."

"What is that?"

"Being ill."

In her continual sufferings, Jesus was her consoler. A look at the crucifix gave her strength. "I am happier upon my bed with my crucifix than a queen upon her throne," she would say. And a short time before her death, after she had given away all that still belonged to her, a few pictures: "I need only that," she said, looking at the crucifix. "That suffices for me."

In addition to asthmatic convulsions, hemorrhage and her lung trouble, she suffered from almost intolerable pain, caused by an abscess, which had formed on her right knee. So intense was her suffering that her countenance became livid. The sisters exhausted every effort to mitigate her torture. "My God, I offer this suffering to Thee; my God, I love Thee," was the unceasing aspiration of Sister Marie-Bernard. To one of her companions who said to her, "Sister, you suffer much," she answered: "It is all good for heaven." "I will ask our Immaculate Mother to give you some relief, said the sister. "No, no, not relief, but strength and patience," she said.

On Wednesday, in Easter week, one hour before her death, raising her eyes to heaven, she cried out with an indefinable expression, more of surprise than of suffering: "Oh! oh! oh!" Did our Immaculate Mother show herself for a last time on earth to the child of her predilection? Sister Marie-Bernard has revealed nothing on this point.

A little later she lovingly kissed her crucifix and said: "I am thirsty." Then she said in a low voice: "Holy Mary, Mother of God, pray for me, a poor sinner—a poor sinner." —The victim, with this prayer to the Immaculate Virgin on her lips sweetly breathed forth her soul. Her death occurred at a quarter past three in the afternoon of April 16th, 1879.

THY LILY, Mother, scents the earth,

Where came thy love to bring it home,
Here make it grow in second birth,
On altar fair decreed by Rome!

FROM HEAVEN THIS "LILY" sheds its perfume upon earth, a perfume which fills many souls with thanksgiving for the favors it has brought them; very many cures, unexpected assistance, conversions both well known and hidden, lives reformed, sufferings alleviated, insurmountable difficulties overcome—all concur in establishing confidence, when prayer is offered to this "Mystic Lily," transplanted in the celestial garden to blossom there eternally.

We cannot here relate these favors; the mere enumeration of them would be too long. "La Confidente de l'Immaculée"—the English translation of which is entitled, "Bernadette of Lourdes"—gives a number of the answers of heaven to the prayers addressed to Bernadette.

26

WORDS OF THE BLESSED VIRGIN TO BERNADETTE

At the third apparition, Thursday, Feb. 18th—Bernadette, presenting to the Blessed Virgin pen and paper and ink, asked her to write down her wishes: *"What I have to say to you it is not necessary that I should put in writing. Would you have the kindness to come here for fifteen days?"* . . . *"I do not promise you that you will be happy in this world but in the other."*

At the sixth apparition, Sunday, Feb. 21st—*"Pray for sinners."*

Seventh apparition, Tuesday, Feb. 23rd—The Blessed Virgin confided a threefold personal secret to Bernadette and added: *"I forbid you to tell this to anyone."* Bernadette has never revealed these secrets.

At the eighth apparition, Wednesday, Feb. 24th—*"Penitence, Penitence, Penitence."*

At the ninth apparition, Thursday, Feb. 25th—*"Go to the spring and drink and wash there."*

At the tenth apparition, Friday, Feb 26th—*"Kiss the earth for sinners."* At the eleventh apparition, Saturday, Feb. 27th—*"Go and tell the priests that a chapel should be built here."*

At the fourteenth apparition, Tuesday, March 2nd—
"The Blessed Virgin again requested Bernadette to go and
tell the priests that a chapel should be built at Massabielle,
and she added: *I desire that people should come here in
procession.*"

NOTES

LETTER TO THE AUTHOR

1. Entitled, in English, Bernadette of Lourdes.